VAN GOGH

BY

DAVID SPENCE

THE ARTIST & HIS TIMES

THE WORLD IN THE 1880S

It was in the year 1880 that Vincent van Gogh decided to become an artist. The world was changing rapidly, with European imperial powers such as Britain and France continuing to colonise new lands. Africa was being divided. The British defeated the Zulus in 1879 and in 1882 France created a French colony in the Congo which was larger than France itself. In 1877 Britain had proclaimed Queen Victoria 'Empress of India', ruthlessly stamping out a mutiny in its most precious colony some 20 years earlier. Prussia, ruled by Otto von Bismarck, had defeated France and was to build the new republic of Germany. By 1890 half a million immigrants were arriving each year in the United States of America. The modern world was in the making with the invention of the telephone by Alexander Graham Bell in 1876, the first ever phonograph recording by Thomas Edison in 1877 and the invention of the electric light bulb. Alexandre Gustave Eiffel built the *Statue of Liberty* in a Paris suburb before it was shipped to New York in 214 cases in 1884, and then became world famous for his *Eiffel Tower.*

PRIDE OF PARIS

In 1889 the engineer Alexandre Gustave Eiffel built this tower, which stands in the heart of Paris, to celebrate the 100th anniversary of the French revolution. It is now famous throughout the world as the Eiffel Tower.

COLLAPSE OF EMPIRE

European powers had already colonised many parts of the world and in the 19th century countries such as Britain, Germany, Russia, Italy and Japan forced China to grant trading rights. This cartoon shows the powers carving up the Chinese cake while the Chinaman looks on in horror.

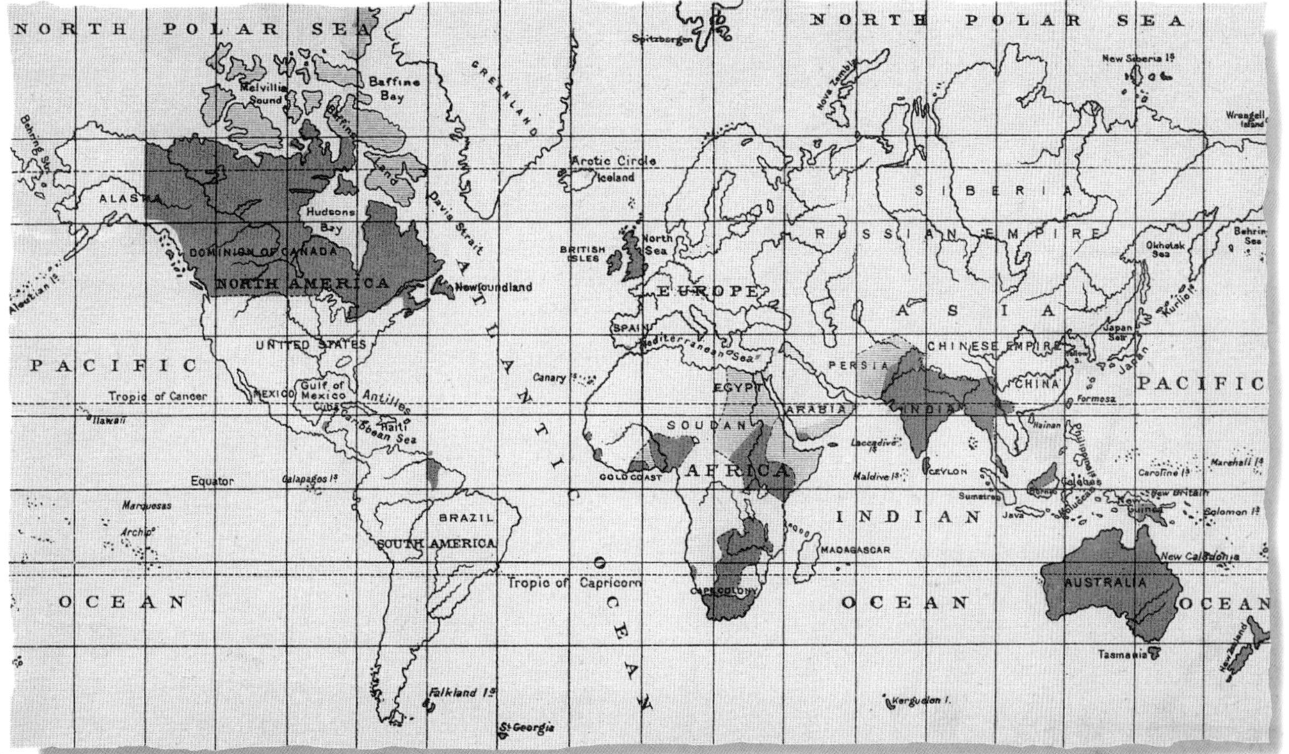

THE ELECTRIC LIGHT BULB

The American Thomas Edison invented the electric light bulb in 1880, making a practical light bulb which glowed brightly as an electric current passed through it. The Englishman Joseph Swan made the same invention independent of Edison in the same year.

BRITANNIA RULES THE WAVES

There were many maps published in the second half of the 19th century which showed British global dominance. The British empire stretched from Canada to Australia by way of India. Because Britain 'ruled the waves' it controlled world trade and was all-powerful. The extent of the empire is shown by those areas coloured red on the map. Germany was soon to challenge Britain's dominance.

THE PACE OF LIFE

The scientific and engineering advances, such as electric lighting, photography and railway networks, began to change the way in which people lived and worked. The pace of life seemed to be getting faster as the century moved towards its close.

THE WORLD OF VINCENT VAN GOGH

Vincent was the son of a Dutch pastor, Theodorus van Gogh. He was born on 30 March 1853 at Zundert, a village in the south Netherlands. Art was a part of Vincent's upbringing because several uncles in the family were art dealers. Art and religion, therefore, were among Vincent's early experiences as he grew up in the family home alongside his three sisters and two brothers. Vincent tried his hand at many things before turning to painting. He worked in the family art dealing business; turned to religion and preached the gospel, and enrolled at the Academy of Fine Art. In 1880, at the age of 27, Vincent suffered intense depression. He had failed in the family's gallery business, failed as a teacher, failed in love and had now failed in his desire to preach the gospel. Vincent now decided to become an artist. *'In spite of everything I shall rise again...'*

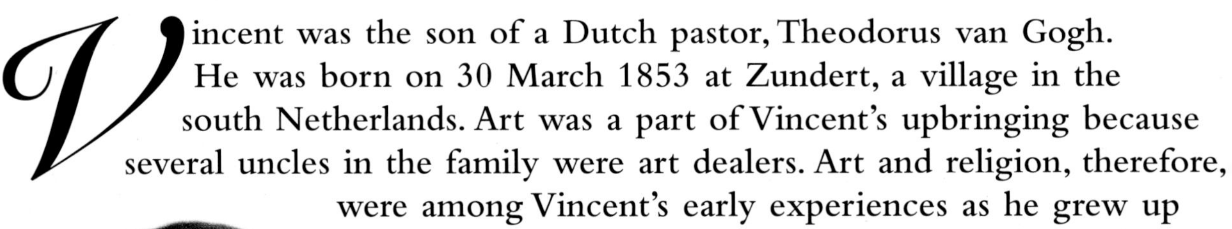

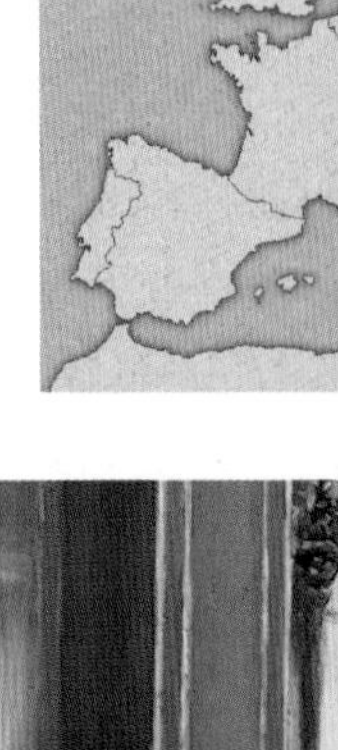

THE YOUNG ARTIST

At the age of 16, Vincent was apprenticed to The Hague branch of Goupil & Cie, a Paris art publisher specialising in printed graphics. Vincent's godfather, 'Uncle Cent', also worked for the firm as did Vincent's brother Theo. Vincent was to work as an art dealer for seven years during which time he worked both in Paris and London. When lodging in London he fell in love with his landlady's daughter, Eugenie Loyer. Her rejection may have been the reason for Vincent's depression and poor work which finally caused his employer to sack him. Vincent turned to religion.

Self-Portrait with Dark Felt Hat, (detail) 1886.

FARMHOUSES, THE HAGUE, 1883

In October 1880 Vincent decided to enrol at the Academy of Fine Art. He failed to impress his teachers and after his brother Theo agreed to support him financially Vincent moved to The Hague to develop his new career as an artist.

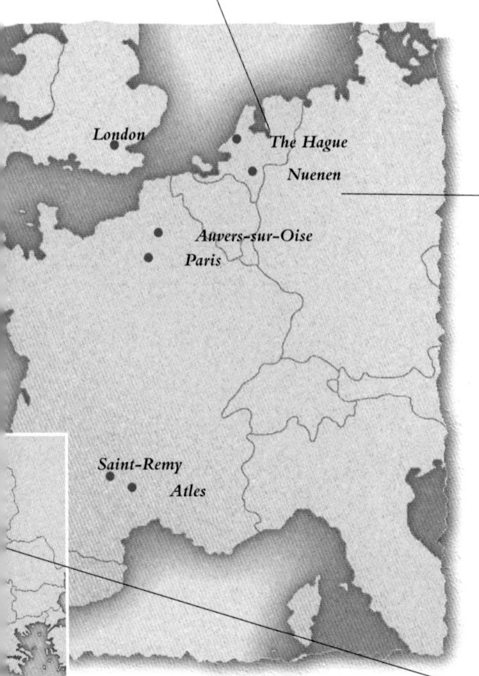

THE PARSONAGE GARDEN AT NUENEN, 1884

Vincent painted obsessively during his years in and around the family home in Nuenen before he finally moved to Paris in 1886. He had little regard for his own well being and would spend his little money on paint rather than food which resulted in him losing nearly all of his teeth. His brother Theo, who already supported him, said '*...now we must wait and see if he has genius... if he succeeds he will be a great man.*'

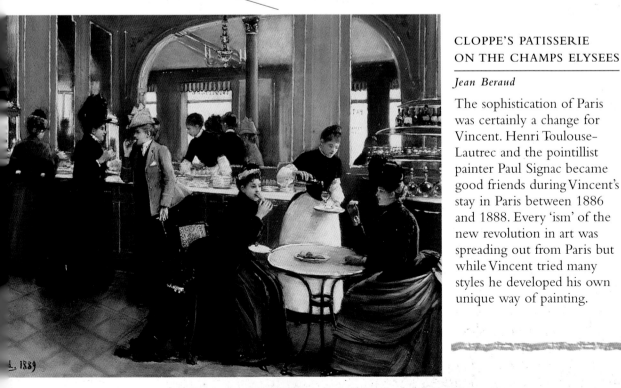

CLOPPE'S PATISSERIE ON THE CHAMPS ELYSEES

Jean Beraud

The sophistication of Paris was certainly a change for Vincent. Henri Toulouse-Lautrec and the pointillist painter Paul Signac became good friends during Vincent's stay in Paris between 1886 and 1888. Every 'ism' of the new revolution in art was spreading out from Paris but while Vincent tried many styles he developed his own unique way of painting.

THE ART OF HIS DAY

Even before Vincent had moved to the cosmopolitan world of Paris he was aware of the artistic trends around him. He said in 1885 *'...there is a school I think of Impressionists, but I do not know much about it'*. It is certain that in his years working with the art dealers Goupil & Cie in The Hague, Paris and London Vincent would have been aware of what was happening in the world of art around him, and in the late 19th century, Paris was at the very centre of that world. When Vincent moved to Paris in 1886 he would have come into contact with many artists through his brother, Theo, who helped sell the paintings of the first real Impressionists such as Monet, Pissarro and Sisley. Vincent himself began experimenting with the *plein air* (open air) way of painting favoured by the Impressionists.

HENRI DE TOULOUSE-LAUTREC

Lautrec came from a noble French family. He suffered from a disability which restricted his growth and he sought solace in the sordid nightlife of Paris. His pictures of nightclub scenes are full of movement, colour and life but are also a ruthless portrayal of the seedy side of Paris life.

Detail from *The Salon Rue des Moulins, 1894.*

GARDEN AT VETHEUIL *Claude Monet*

By the time Vincent came to Paris, Claude Monet was 46 years old and already an artist with a reputation. His painting *Impression, Sunrise* after which the Impressionist movement was named had been painted some 13 years earlier. The influence of the Impressionist painters led Vincent to experiment with colour and 'plein air' painting.

THE BATHERS *Georges Seurat*

Seurat developed an optical style of painting called *Pointillism* which used dots of colour laid beside one another. When these coloured dots were viewed from a distance they blended together 'mixing' the colours in the viewer's eye rather than on the canvas. Seurat's fellow pointillist Paul Signac was a good friend of Vincent who borrowed from this style of art in some of his own paintings.

CARNATION, LILY, LILY, ROSE

John Singer Sargent

Sargent was an American artist who trained in Paris but worked in England. Best known for his society portrait pictures, Sargent was aware of and sometimes adopted Impressionist principles such as 'plein air' painting.

GRANDMOTHER READING TO CHILDREN

Mary Cassatt

The two outstanding women Impressionist painters were Berthe Morisot and Mary Cassatt. Cassatt was an American who came to Paris in 1868 in order to paint. Her enthusiasm for Japanese prints was shared by Vincent. She was an accomplished print-maker and produced a set of prints using Japanese techniques. Many of Cassatt's pictures were of domestic scenes because women were not as free as men to paint in the public cafés and boulevards of Paris.

FAMILY & FRIENDS

Vincent relied heavily on his family and friends to support him throughout his life as an artist. It was his brother, Theo, who agreed to support him financially when at the age of 28 Vincent decided to learn how to paint. That support continued until Vincent's death. His love affair with painting was intense and painful, just as his earlier passions for the Church and his unsuccessful relationships with women had been.

PÈRE TANGUY, 1887

Vincent bought his paint from Julien Tanguy' store in Paris. Tanguy, an idealist and former Communard, considered that Vincent and his fellow artists deserved support. Sometimes Vince exchanged his paintings for supplies of Tanguy paint. The little back room of Tanguy's store doubled as a gallery and some of the artists we consider today to be the founders of 20th-centu art such as van Gogh, Seurat and Cézanne exhibited their pictures with Père Tanguy.

NEVERMORE

Paul Gauguin

Gauguin did not share Vincent's vision of an artist's community dedicated to work (*you must live like a monk who goes to a brothel every other week,* he told another artist friend). Two years after leaving Vincent, Gauguin left France for Tahiti in pursuit of his own dreams. His escape to the South Sea Islands gave him personal freedom from European social conventions and this freedom is reflected in his paintings which are not bound by the naturalistic conventions of the day.

DOCTOR GACHET, 1890

Paul Gachet was a close friend of Vincent and collected his paintings. His support persuaded Vincent to move to Gachet's home town of Auvers-sur-Oise, near Paris, in May 1890. After the terrible depression and periods of insanity in Arles, Vincent gained a new lease of life in Auvers with the help of Gachet. Not only did Gachet provide friendship but he also convinced Vincent of the value of his work.

VINCENT'S BROTHER, THEO

Vincent's brother was an art dealer in Paris. He regularly sent money from his own income to Vincent to allow him to paint. Theo was devoted to Vincent and christened his own son, born in January 1890, Vincent Willem. Theo was devastated by Vincent's death and survived him by only 6 months, dying on 25 January 1891.

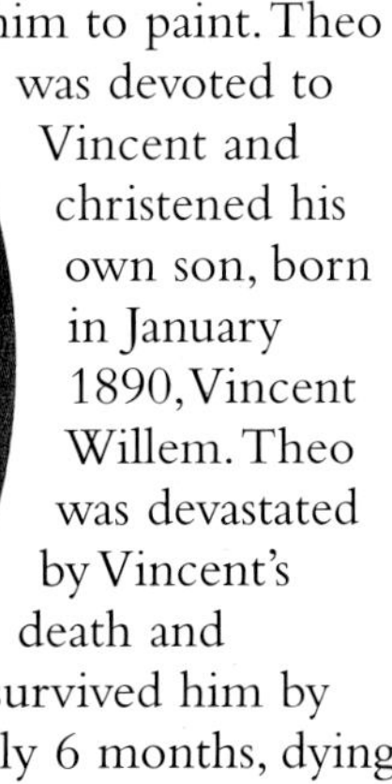

The Life of van Gogh

~March 30 1852~
A son is stillborn to Theodorus and Anna van Gogh. They name him Vincent

~March 30 1853~
Another son is born. Theodorus and Anna name him Vincent

~1857~
Vincent's brother, Theo, is born

~1869~
Vincent is apprenticed to the Paris art dealers Goupil & Cie

~1873~
Transferred to London branch of Goupil & Cie. Vincent falls in love with his landlady's daughter, Eugenie Loyer. She rejects him

~1876~
Vincent is sacked from Goupil & Cie. He travels to Ramsgate in England where he gets a job as an assistant teacher. School moves to London and Vincent takes up preaching at Richmond Methodist Church

~1880~
Moves to Brussels to enrol at the Academy of Fine Art but doesn't stay

~April 1881~
Returns to parents' home in Etten where he falls in love with his cousin Kee Vos. She rejects him

~November 1881~
Moves to The Hague and takes up painting lessons. Falls in love with alcoholic prostitute Sien Hoornik. He lives with Sien and her daughter

The Life of van Gogh

~1883~

Vincent leaves Sien

~1884~

Relationship with Margot Begemann, a neighbour, ends with her attempted suicide

~1885~

Vincent's father dies. Paints *The Potato Eaters*. Moves to Antwerp and enrols in the Academy of Fine Art but teachers reject his work

~1886~

Moves in with Theo in Paris. Theo introduces Vincent to the work of Monet, Renoir and other Impressionists. Gauguin becomes a good friend

~February 1888~

Moves to Arles in the south of France and dreams of starting an artist's colony

~September 1888~

Seen painting at night, in the town, with candles fixed to his hat

~October 1888~

Gauguin joins Vincent in Arles

~23 December 1888~

Gauguin decides to leave Arles. Vincent threatens Gauguin with a razor. Gauguin leaves. Vincent cuts off his earlobe with the razor, wraps it in newspaper and gives it to Rachel, a prostitute in a nearby brothel. Theo visits Vincent in hospital

~February 1989~

Vincent taken to hospital suffering from hallucinations. Vincent paints portrait with bandaged ear

FISHING IN THE SPRING, PONT DE CLICHY, 1887

When Vincent moved to Paris in March 1886 his painting style was descriptive. By the time this painting was executed in Spring 1887 he had developed the use of colour, his paintings clearly showing the influence of artists such as Monet, Seurat and Toulouse-Lautrec with whom he mixed. During his stay in Paris he painted over 200 pictures, averaging more than two per week.

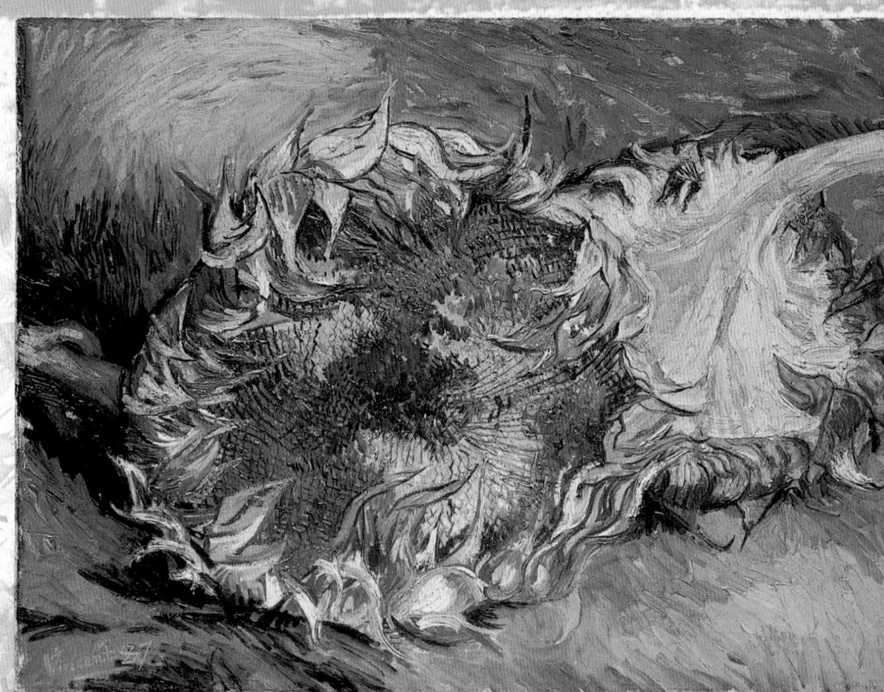

TWO CUT SUNFLOWERS, 1887

In the Summer of 1887 Vincent painted his first sunflower pictures. Sunflowers fascinated him; the bright splash of sensuous yellow, the colour of sunlight, warmth and friendship. Sunflowers were to remain a favourite subject for him and he painted them many times. In a letter dated August 1888 when in Arles and anticipating Gauguin's arrival he writes *'Now that I hope to live with Gauguin in a studio of our own, I want to make a decoration for the studio. Nothing but big sunflowers'*. Vincent refers to the sunflower as *'...somewhat my own'*.

LETTERS HOME

Vincent's letters to his family and friends form a unique record of his life. He wrote regularly to his brother Theo and it is mainly through the existence of this correspondence that we know so much about him today. Vincent stayed with Theo in Paris from March 1886 to February 1888 and of course had no need to send letters to him. As a consequence we know far less about Vincent's life during this period than any other. When he moved to Arles he sent letters every week to Theo and this correspondence describes his struggle with himself and his art.

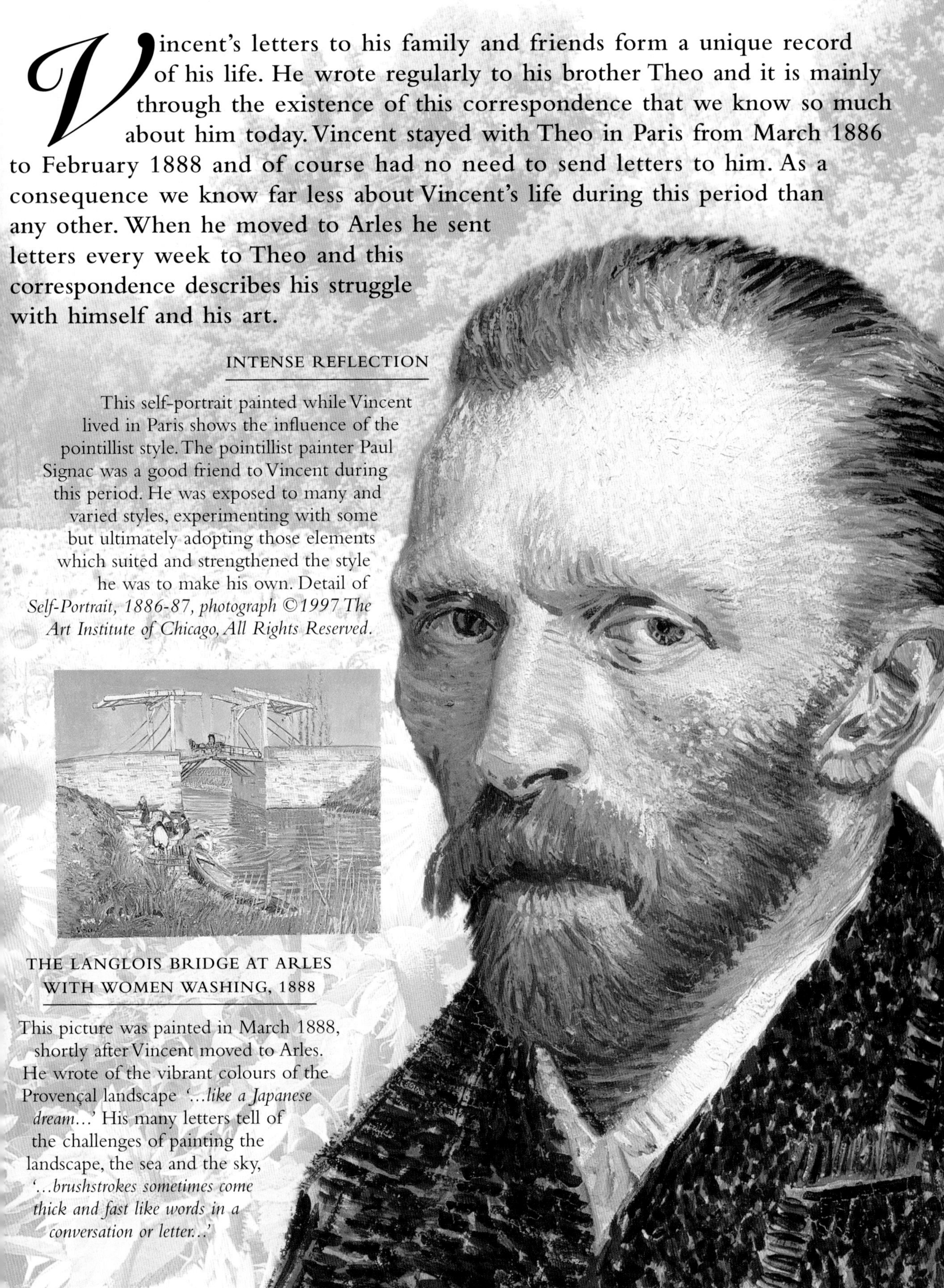

INTENSE REFLECTION

This self-portrait painted while Vincent lived in Paris shows the influence of the pointillist style. The pointillist painter Paul Signac was a good friend to Vincent during this period. He was exposed to many and varied styles, experimenting with some but ultimately adopting those elements which suited and strengthened the style he was to make his own. Detail of *Self-Portrait, 1886-87, photograph ©1997 The Art Institute of Chicago, All Rights Reserved.*

THE LANGLOIS BRIDGE AT ARLES WITH WOMEN WASHING, 1888

This picture was painted in March 1888, shortly after Vincent moved to Arles. He wrote of the vibrant colours of the Provençal landscape *'...like a Japanese dream...'* His many letters tell of the challenges of painting the landscape, the sea and the sky, *'...brushstrokes sometimes come thick and fast like words in a conversation or letter...'*

THE FINAL STRUGGLE

'I wish it were all over now...' It is impossible to read the letters written by Vincent towards the end of his life without a deep feeling of sorrow. His illness brought extended periods of madness when he experienced hallucinations complete with voices and visions, but between these attacks he was perfectly well and acutely aware of his condition.
In September 1889 he writes *'During the attacks I feel a coward before the pain and suffering... altogether I am now trying to recover like a man who has meant to commit suicide and, finding the water too cold, tries to regain the bank'.*
This was an indication of what was later to happen. Vincent shot himself on 27 July 1890, dying two days later. His last, unfinished letter to Theo was found on his body and reads *'Well my own work, I am risking my life for it...'* Some think he planned his death in order to increase the value of his work and thereby repay his brother, with whom he had had an arrangement since 1884 that all paintings sent to Theo were Theo's property in exchange for the monthly allowance paid to Vincent. Whatever his motive Theo observed *'He has found the peace he never found on earth'.*

THATCHED COTTAGES BY A HILL, 1890

Vincent painted this picture in July 1890. He found the village of Auvers *'... very beautiful, among other things a lot of old thatched roofs, which are getting rare'.* He was happy in Auvers despite the tragic end to his life.

WHEAT FIELD UNDER CLOUDED SKY, 1890

'They are infinitely vast wheat fields beneath a dismal sky... and I have not shied away from the attempt to express sadness and extreme loneliness... I almost believe these pictures will communicate to you what I am unable to put into words.'

BROTHERS IN DEATH

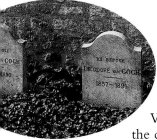

Theo arrived on 28 July and sat with Vincent until the end. Vincent's coffin lay in a room hung with all of his last paintings and surrounded by flowers, including, of course, sunflowers. Theo died within months of Vincent and they were buried side by side in the cemetery at Auvers.

THE LIFE OF VAN GOGH

~MAY 1889~
Voluntarily enters mental asylum at St Rémy

~JULY 1889~
Has another attack while painting outdoors and loses memory as a result of unconsciousness

~3 SEPTEMBER 1889~
Paintings exhibited at the Salon des Indépendants, Paris

~DECEMBER 1889~
Suffers more attacks and tries to poison himself by swallowing paint

~JANUARY 1890~
Paintings exhibited at Les Vingt, Brussels. The first and only painting to be sold in his lifetime, *The Red Vineyard*, bought for 400 francs

~MARCH 1890~
Ten paintings exhibited at Salon des Indépendants. Monet considers Vincent's paintings to be the best in the show.

~MAY 1890~
Moves to Auvers-sur-Oise to be near Dr Gachet. Paints 80 paintings

~27 JULY 1890~
Goes out for an evening walk and shoots himself in the chest. Returns home to his room at Ravoux's café where Dr Gachet bandages him and puts him to bed. Spends all the next day in bed smoking his pipe. Theo arrives to comfort him

~29 JULY 1890~
Vincent dies on the night of 29 July and is buried the next day.

Vincent's 'yellow house' was influenced by his enthusiasm for Japanese art. The print on the wall is by Toyokuni and is of Japanese Geishas. Yellow signified the sunshine of the South but also the welcome he always sought. He wrote when travelling South to Arles *'I can still remember vividly how excited I became that winter when travelling from Paris to Arles. How I was constantly on the lookout to see if we had reached Japan yet.'*

SELF-PORTRAIT WITH BANDAGED EAR, 1889

One of Vincent's most famous paintings, showing him shortly after he had cut off his ear lobe. This was painted in his 'yellow house' in Arles.

BLOSSOMING ALMOND TREE, 1890

Painted while in the asylum in St Rémy in February 1890 and only months before his death, this simple picture of almond blossom was painted as a present to his brother on the birth of Theo's son, also named Vincent. The picture clearly shows the influence of the Japanese style.

The Artist's Vision

WHAT DO THE PAINTINGS SAY?

Japan's borders had been closed to foreigners for hundreds of years until the 1850s when it was forced to start trading with the outside world. In the Paris World Fair of 1867 Japanese design came to France. At about the same time Japanese prints started to find their way to Europe along with shipped goods. The prints were often used as cheap wrapping paper by the Japanese for whom the prints held no value. Japanese art appeared very exotic to European eyes. The strong colours, decorative design and flattened perspective became fashionable with European artists, and Vincent was no exception.

PORTRAIT OF AN ACTOR *Toyokuni Go*

Vincent collected Japanese prints avidly, spending time rowsing in a shop which sold prints near his Montmartre flat. His collection eventually grew to around 400 hundred prints.

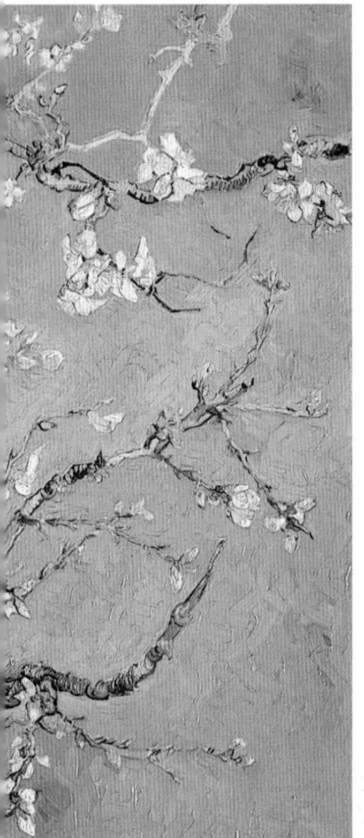

JAPONAISERIE: FLOWERING PLUM TREE, 1887

Vincent painted this picture in 1887, while he was living in Paris. The craze for Japanese art affected many but for Vincent it assumed a special importance. He built up a large collection of prints and believed that Japanese art represented a more profound way to depict nature. He began to think that the bright colours and strong light of the South of France would offer a 'second Japan' for him.

...WHAT DO THE PAINTINGS SAY...

'I am tremendously gripped by the problem of painting night scenes or nighttime effects on the spot, actually at night' wrote Vincent. Night scenes appealed to him just as much as the colourful Provence landscape that he had dreamed of and was reality when he moved to Arles in February 1888. In a letter he wrote *'Death may possibly not be the hardest thing in the life of a painter. I must declare I know nothing about them, but when I look at the stars I always start dreaming, as readily as when the black points that indicate towns and villages on a map always start me dreaming. Why, I wonder, should the shining points of the heavens be less accessible to us than the black dots on a map of France? Just as we take a train to reach Tarascon or Rouen, we use death in order to reach a star.'*

STARRY NIGHT OVER THE RHONE, 1888

Vincent painted this night scene almost a year before his now world famous *Starry Night*. The intensity of the starlight rivals that of the artificial light shining from the buildings on the riverside.

The couple in the foreground are similar to the couple in *Landscape with Couple Walking and Crescent Moon*. In both cases Vincent appears to have given the man red hair, suggesting that the figure may be himself. In his pictures he has the partner he never found in life.

The figure standing behind the table is described by Vincent as 'the landlord'. This would be Monsieur Ginoux. His white clothes are painted a lemon yellow reflecting the lighting from the 'four lemon -yellow lamps'.

THE NIGHT CAFÉ IN THE PLACE LAMARTINE IN ARLES, 1888

When he arrived in Arles, Vincent lodged in the café at the Place Lamartine, his room over the bar depicted here. His letter to his brother Theo describes the intention behind the painting. Vincent writes *'I have tried to express the terrible passions of humanity by means of red and green. The room is blood red and dark yellow with a green billiard table in the middle.'*

A couple sit together, lost in each other and oblivious to the slumped, drunken figures who make up the rest of Ginoux's clientele. The clock above the bar shows a quarter-past midnight.

THE CAFÉ TERRACE ON THE PLACE DU FORUM, ARLES, AT NIGHT, 1888

The glare of gaslight fills the café canopy with 'sulphur yellow and limey green' in this picture painted by Vincent after he had set up his easel in the square at night. He describes *'... a night picture without any black, nothing but beautiful blue and violet and green...'*

It is a warm September evening in Arles and a dozen people sit out on the café terrace, the waiter moves amongst them. On the cobbled streets figures stroll under the brilliant starry sky.

WHAT DO THE PAINTINGS SAY

The reaper is 'the image of death as the great book of nature represents it to us'. Vincent's letter of September 1889 to Theo says *'... already I can see myself in the future, when I shall have had some success, regretting my solitude and wretchedness here, when I saw between the iron bars of the cell the reaper in the field below. Misfortune is good for something'.*

When Vincent moved to Arles he had hoped to set up an artist's colony. By December 1888 all hope faded as he quarrelled with his good friend Gauguin who had come to join him. Alone once again and suffering from fits of depression and actual breakdown, Vincent became a voluntary patient in the asylum at St Rémy, living in two rooms paid for by his brother Theo. He continued to suffer breakdowns until the end of his life. His pictures are full of emotional intensity as he struggles to paint during periods of calm between the distress of his delusional fits.

THE GARDEN OF SAINT PAUL'S HOSPITAL, ST RÉMY, 1889

Theo paid 800 francs a year for Vincent's stay at the asylum at St Rémy, near Arles. The building, originally a monastery, was known at the time for its enlightened treatment of the sick. Vincent had two rooms, a bedroom and a studio.

THE REAPER

Vincent was not confined to the asylum and once his confidence returned he went out into the surrounding countryside to paint. At first he painted the nearby fields then a little further out, to the hills and cypress trees. *Enclosed Wheat Field with Reaper, 1889.*

WHEAT FIELD WITH CROWS, 1890

In May 1890 Vincent moved to Auvers-sur-Oise, near Paris, to be near Theo. He painted this dark, broody picture of crows struggling in a stormy sky just days before he committed suicide. During the two months at Auvers before his death Vincent painted 70 pictures.

SELF-PORTRAIT, 1889

This picture, painted in September 1889 while at the asylum, is merciless in its self-examination. The eyes, penetrating in their gaze, appear to look deep inside the viewer. Vincent worked during periods of clear thinking and calm between bouts of depression and fits of insanity during which he tried to poison himself by eating his paint.

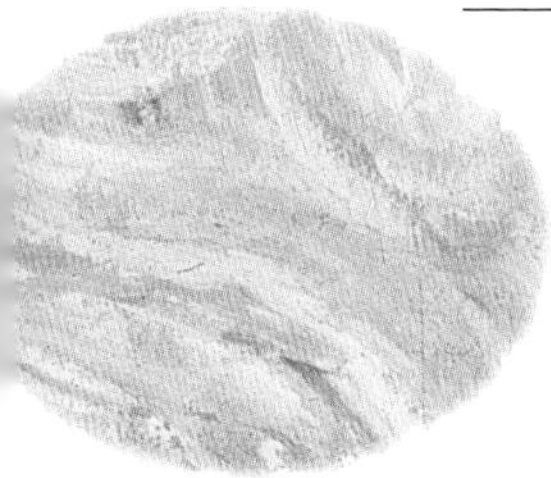

The swirling blue and white lines of the background hint at the sea of instability in which he felt he lived, the chaos of his existence. His bedroom at the asylum had green wallpaper and curtains described by Vincent as 'sea-green'.

Vincent wrote *'I am in a cage, I am in a cage, and I've got everything I need, fools! I've got everything I could possibly want! Ah dear God, freedom - to be a bird like the other birds.'*

HOW WERE THEY MADE?

'My dear Theo, Thank you very much for sending me the canvas and paints which have just arrived... if on the 10 metres of canvas I paint only masterpieces half a metre in size and sell them cash down and at an exorbitant price... nothing will be easier than to make a fortune on this consignment'.

It was difficult for Vincent to get good paints, canvas and brushes locally when in the South of France. Theo sent him supplies to keep up with his rapid production of pictures, sometimes several in a day. By this time commercially produced artist's paints were available in tin or lead tubes enabling artists to transport their materials easily, especially important for painting outdoors, which Vincent often did. He would apply paint thickly (impasto), sometimes using a knife rather than brushes, as the mood would take him. Black lines, adopted from the Japanese style, can be seen in his paintings. This helped to set his art apart from the 'true' Impressionists who banished black from their palette.

CANDLE POWER

Vincent is reported to have attached candles to his easel and even to the brim of his hat in order to help him paint out in the open at night.

TOOLS OF THE TRADE

Vincent was dependent on Theo for supplies of artist's materials which he sent regularly according to Vincent's needs. In June 1889, Vincent wrote to Theo from St Rémy,

'My Dear Theo,
I must beg you again to send me as soon as possible some ordinary brushes... Half a dozen of each, please; I hope that you are well and your wife too, and that you are enjoying the fine weather a little. Here at any rate we have splendid sunshine. As for me, my health is good, and as for my brain, that will be, let us hope, a matter of time and patience'.

Vase with Irises against a Yellow Background, 1890.

THE COLOURS OF NATURE

When Vincent was in the asylum at St Rémy he was free to go into the garden of the asylum and paint. His studies of lilacs and irises demonstrate that his attraction to the blues and violets of these plants was as compelling as his attraction to the yellows of sunflowers. The deep black outlines filled with vivid blues and use of varnish to highlight the luminous colours make the pictures glow as if they were stained-glass windows. These subjects served to combine Vincent's passion for colour with his abiding interest in nature. When Vincent left St Rémy the director, Dr Peyron, said in his final report: 'The patient, who was calm on the whole, suffered a number of violent attacks during his stay at the asylum, lasting from a week to a month. During these attacks he was overcome by terrible fears and anxieties, and repeatedly tried to poison himself, either by swallowing paint or by drinking kerosene stolen from the assistants... Between these attacks the patient was absolutely quiet, and devoted himself entirely to his painting'.

FAMOUS IMAGES

VINCENT'S CHAIR WITH HIS PIPE, 1888

Vincent painted this picture, together with one called *Paul Gauguin's Armchair*, in December 1888 shortly before Gauguin left. Vincent's simple peasant chair is painted yellow, the colour of sunshine and warmth, even though it was made of white wood. This symbolic colouring of surfaces is quite typical of his painting. Vincent's pipe and tobacco are on the empty chair. In contrast on Gauguin's chair rest books and a candlestick complete with burning candle. This may allude to the flame of friendship which Vincent feared would soon be extinguished.

Vincent planned to start an artist's community in the South of France, and when his wealthy art dealer Uncle Cent died and left Vincent money it was immediately used to refurbish the rented rooms in the yellow house in Arles. Vincent invited Gauguin to live with him in the yellow house, and Gauguin was persuaded, not by Vincent but his brother Theo who represented Gauguin's work in the Paris galleries. Gauguin agreed to stay with Vincent as long as Theo gave him a financial allowance. Gauguin arrived in October 1888 but it seems they did not get on well despite Vincent's great need for a companion. Gauguin left just two months later on 23 December.

VINCENT'S BEDROOM IN ARLES, 1889

When Vincent knew Gauguin was to come to his yellow house he set about preparing it for his friend. He painted many pictures which were hung on the walls of the house and used to decorate Gauguin's room. This picture of Vincent's bedroom is one of two copies he made in St Rémy from an original painted in October 1888 while Vincent was waiting for his friend to arrive. Vincent regarded it as one of his best pictures, describing it in a letter to Theo *'In a word, to look at the picture ought to rest the brain or rather the imagination.'* The picture has become one of the most famous icons in art, its graphic simplicity underlining the humble way of life it depicts. In many ways this picture epitomises the notion of the romantic artist who cares for nothing except his art.

On the table stand two jugs of water, two bottles, two brushes. Either side of the table stand two chairs. Some consider this pairing an anticipation of his friend's arrival, or perhaps something even deeper; his longing for companionship. It echoes his *Starry Night Over the Rhône* and *Landscape with Couple Walking and Crescent Moon* where Vincent paints himself arm in arm with a companion.

The pictures vary in the different versions, but here they show a self-portrait and a portrait of his sister, Wil. Above the head of the bed hangs a Japanese print.

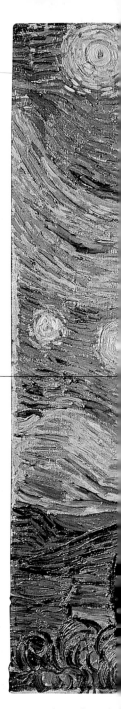

FAMOUS IMAGES

There was an uneasy relationship between Gauguin and Vincent during the two months in Arles. On 23 December Vincent wrote to Theo saying '*I think myself that Gauguin was a little out of sorts with the good town of Arles, the little yellow house where we work, and especially with me... I think that he will definitely go, or else definitely stay.*' Gauguin had in fact already made up his mind to go. Vincent's agitation, caused by the prospect of losing his friend, only served to push Gauguin over the edge and he walked out on the evening of the 23rd. Vincent was unable to cope with this sudden loss and in a state of emotional turmoil he cut off his earlobe with a razor, wrapped it in a handkerchief then walked to the local brothel where he presented the bizarre gift to a prostitute before returning home, where he lapsed into unconsciousness.

Why did Vincent go to the brothel and present a prostitute with his earlobe? Having lost his friend he turned to those who he felt understood him. Artists and prostitutes alike were rejected by society and Vincent felt a kinship with the social outcasts.

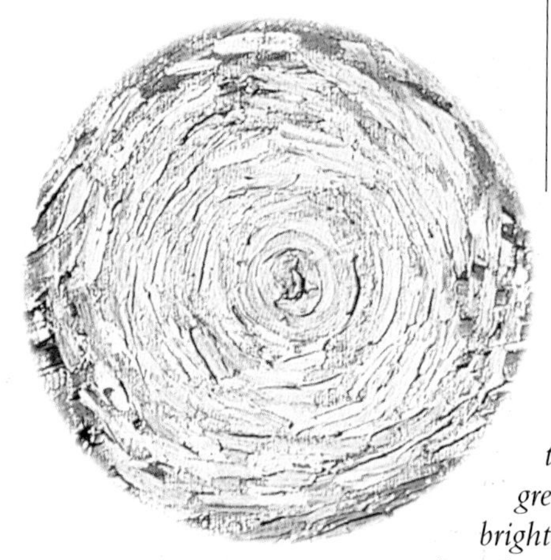

Vincent describes the night sky in a letter to Theo '*In the blue depth the stars were sparkling, greenish yellow, white, rose, brighter, flashing more like jewe[ls] than they do at home - even in Pari[s]. opals you might call them, emeralds, lapis, rubies, sapphire[s].*'

SELF-PORTRAIT WITH BANDAGED EAR, 1889

The most famous of Vincent's self-portraits shows him back in the yellow house after being treated in hospital following his self-mutilation. Had the prostitute not called the police, who found Vincent at home, he would have bled to death. This was the first of many periods of insanity which plagued Vincent until his death.

THE STARRY NIGHT, 1889

In April 1889 Vincent enters the asylum of St-Paul-de-Mausole at St Rémy. Here he is allowed to paint, and to take his paints and easel into the surrounding countryside of olive groves, hills and tall cypresses black against the bleached landscape of a southern summer. It is perhaps strange but not surprising that what has become the most famous of Vincent's paintings, *The Starry Night*, was painted from memory.

The landscape upon which the viewer looks is made from the elements that surrounded Vincent in his asylum; the cluster of olive trees, the little village with church spire and the bold dark shape of the cypress tree. However it is the sky that is overpowering with swirling sea-like lines interspersed with stars exploding like bright fireworks; and the moon, typically painted in Vincent's favourite yellow, glowing in the night sky.

JOSEPH ROULIN, 1889

Roulin and Vincent were the closest of friends. It was Roulin, the local postman, who had helped Vincent home from the brothel after he had mutilated his ear on that fateful night in December 1888. When Vincent was recuperating in hospital Roulin visited him every day, and Roulin's sons sent reports on Vincent's progress to Theo in Paris because Roulin was unable to write.

LA BERCEUSE (AUGUSTINE ROULIN), 1889

Augustine was the wife of Joseph Roulin and they were neighbours of Vincent in Arles. Vincent painted Joseph, Augustine and their children. In this painting Augustine can be seen holding a rope, the other end of which was tied to a cradle. By pulling the rope she could rock her baby in its cradle while sitting still for Vincent. As payment for her efforts Vincent allowed her to choose from three portraits he made of her.

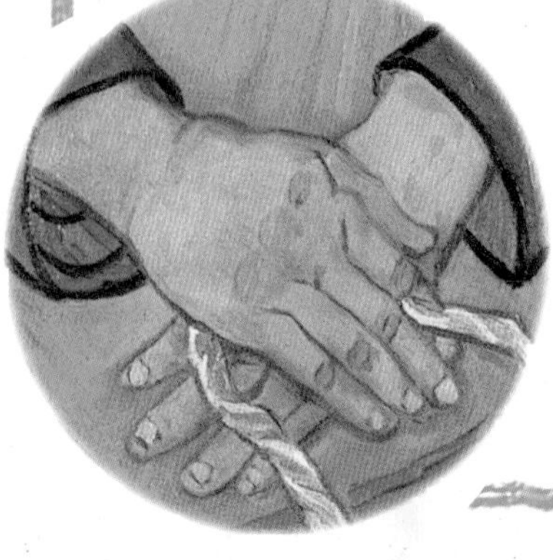

THE RED VINEYARD, 1888

Vincent writes in a letter dated November 1888 *'...I'm working now on a vineyard all purple and yellow.'* As before, his colours serve to emphasise the overall impression and feeling of the scene. Figures harvest the grapes amid the burning reds of the vines under a merciless sun. In February of the following year Theo writes to tell him that Anne Boch has bought the painting in Brussels for the sum of 400 francs. It now hangs in the Pushkin Museum in Moscow.

THE AUDIENCE FOR THE PICTURES

We know of just one picture sold in Vincent's lifetime, *The Red Vineyard*, painted in 1888, apart from some of his early paintings which were bought by a junk dealer and sold for a few centimes. Those that did not sell were burned. He did however exhibit his paintings, especially towards the end of his life when he was beginning to be known in the galleries in Paris thanks to the efforts of his brother. Three of his paintings were exhibited at the Salon des Artistes Indépendants in Paris in 1888. In 1889 he exhibited pictures in at least two different shows in Brussels as well as the Salon des Indépendants in Paris.

SELF-PORTRAIT

Paul Gauguin

Despite their differences Gauguin was close to Vincent and an admirer of his work. Gauguin kept with him two of Vincent's sunflower paintings, and when he was in Tahiti even ordered sunflower seeds n order that he might cultivate he plants and then paint them. The association with Vincent can never have been far from his mind.

THE ARTIST'S INFLUENCE

WHAT THE CRITICS SAY

Vincent entered the Academy in Antwerp in 1886 but was at odds with the academic style of tuition, and moved to Paris to be a pupil at the studio of Fernand Cormon, although he stayed only a few months. The Antwerp Academy thought Vincent's work suitable only for the beginners class. As his work developed so it became more appreciated. Fellow artists such as Toulouse-Lautrec, Signac, Monet and Gauguin eventually acknowledged Vincent's ability but initially only his brother Theo and close friends recognised his talent. Gradually, as a few paintings were exhibited here and there, his art received wider recognition. As early as two years after his death a large retrospective exhibition of his work was held, and his fame grew rapidly.

HENRI DE TOULOUSE-LAUTREC

Lautrec studied at the studio of Fernand Cormon and it was through this connection that he knew Vincent. The two became friends and Vincent's painting was to influence Lautrec. It is said that his admiration for Vincent even led Lautrec to challenge to a duel an artist who had spoken ill of Vincent's work.

MERCVRE DE FRANCE

LES ISOLÉS

—★—

:NCENT VAN GOGH

tout à coup, dés la rentrée dans l'ignoble
ıx de la rue sale et de la laide vie réelie,
tèrent, malgré moi, ces bribes de vers en ma

vranto monotonic
ıétal, du marbre et de l'eau....
ıt, méme la coulour noire,
lait fourbi, clair, irisé;
uide enchàssait sa gloire
le rayon cristallisé.....
s cataractes pesantes
ıe des rideaux de cristal
spendaient, éblouissantes,
marailles de métal....

MERCURE DE FRANCE

In January 1890 an article about Vincent's painting by Parisian art critic Albert Aurier appeared in the French newspaper *Mercure de France*. It was full of praise for the artist.

DOCTOR FELIX REY, 1889

Dr Rey was the doctor who treated Vincent when he arrived at the hospital after he had cut off part of his ear. Dr Rey was extremely sympathetic and told Theo he would look after Vincent, adding that he was separated from his own brother and understood Theo's worries. Vincent painted this picture of him some weeks later but Dr Rey was unimpressed and used the picture to block a hole in his chicken shed!

RECOGNITION

Vincent van Gogh is recognised today as one of the greatest painters in the history of European art. The value of his paintings started to increase from the moment of his death. By the 1980's one of the paintings he made of the *The Poet's Garden* (left), was sold in New York for $5.2 million. This picture was one of several painted by Vincent and intended to decorate the walls of Gauguin's room in anticipation of his arrival in Arles. Now when auction houses such as Christie's (right) and Sotheby's sell van Gogh pictures the whole world knows about it.

THE ARTIST'S INFLUENCE

A LASTING IMPRESSION

The influence of Vincent's art has been far reaching and profound. Vincent wrote '*... instead of trying to reproduce exactly what I see before my eyes, I use colour more arbitrarily so as to express myself more forcibly.*' His dramatic use of colour to convey emotion directly influenced artistic movements such as the Fauvists and the Expressionists, and the effects have rippled through much of 20th-century art.

PORTRAIT OF JOHANNA BONGER

Johanna was Theo's wife. It is thanks to her that we know so much about Vincent's life because she kept all of Vincent's letters to Theo when he died. Johanna transcribed the letters which Theo had kept so faithfully and which spanned 18 years of Vincent's life. In all about 670 letters survive. Since their first publication in 1914 the letters have been published many times in different edited forms.

THE POOL OF LONDON *André Derain*

Derain was one of the artists who belonged to a style called Fauvism, although no formal group was ever formed. Fauvists such as Vlaminck and Derain became aware of Vincent's work when it became more widely exhibited after 1901. Vincent's use of colour was taken further by the Fauves who expressed themselves directly through colour. Matisse was one of their number and was to develop colour and shape to abstraction.

THE MONEY MACHINE

Today Vincent is big business. Merchandising is created from his pictures all over the world and across a wide range of products. His paintings can be seen in over 25 major museums and galleries in 10 different countries.

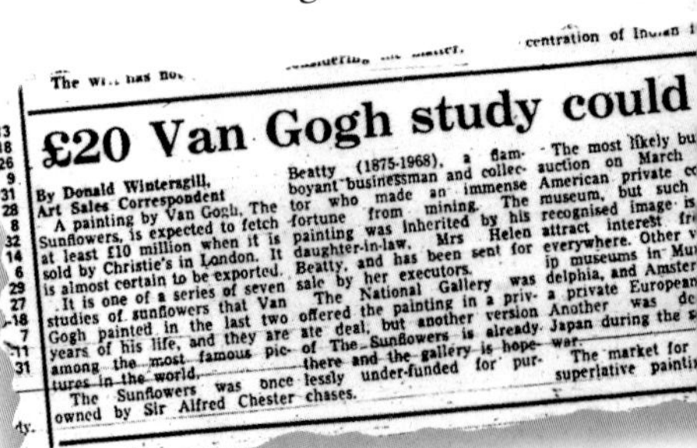

£20 Van Gogh study could

By Donald Wintergill, Art Sales Correspondent

A painting by Van Gogh, The Sunflowers, is expected to fetch at least £10 million when it is sold by Christie's in London. It is almost certain to be exported.

It is one of a series of seven studies of sunflowers that Van Gogh painted in the last two years of his life, and they are among the most famous pictures in the world.

The Sunflowers was once owned by Sir Alfred Chester Beatty (1875-1968), a flamboyant businessman and collector who made an immense fortune from mining. The painting was inherited by his daughter-in-law, Mrs Helen Beatty, and has been sent for sale by her executors.

The National Gallery was offered the painting in a private deal, but another version of The Sunflowers is already there and the gallery is hopelessly under-funded for purchases.

The most likely bu
auction on March
American private c
museum, but such
recognised image is
attract interest fr
everywhere. Other
ip museums in Mu
delphia, and Amster
a private European
Another was de
Japan during the
war.

The market for
superlative painti

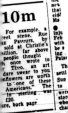

VINCENT'S FAVOURITE SUBJECT

Vincent painted sunflowers again and again during his lifetime. The association between the flower and the artist is now so close that it is not surprising that when one of the sunflower paintings came up for sale in 1989 it fetched the highest price ever paid for a painting. It was sold through Sotheby's to the Yasuda Fire & Marine Insurance Company, Tokyo, and the sale made headlines around the world. *Vase with Fourteen Sunflowers, 1888.*

GLOSSARY

Communard - A Communard was a member of the Paris Commune that fought against the French army in 1871 following the Franco-Prussian war. The Commune was ruthlessly suppressed leading to the death of over 20,000 Communards. Vincent's friend and supplier of art materials 'Père' Julien Tanguy was a former Communard.

Gauguin - Vincent's friend, Paul Gauguin, developed a style of painting which rejected naturalistic representation in favour of expressing mood and emotion through bright colours separated by black lines. He called this Synthetism, which was a kind of symbolism in art.

Icon - Icon originates from the Greek word for image, and originally meant a picture of a Saint or Christ. The rules for painting icons remained the same for nearly 1,000 years. The word has gradually come to mean an image or picture which represents more than it apparently depicts.

Impasto - An Italian word which has found its way into common use as a term to describe the thickness of paint on the surface of a painting. When paint is applied so thickly that it stands proud of the surface and brush marks are clearly evident it is said to be 'impasted' or impasto.

Plein Air - This translates from the French as 'open air'. Until the Impressionist painters of the 1860s, it was virtually unheard of for artists to take their canvas and paints out of the studio and paint outside. Impressionists such as Monet attempted to capture the 'impression' of open air in their pictures.

Salon des Artistes Indépendants - The Salon was originally the only place of exhibition for artists. During the 17th century the venue was the Salon d'Apollon in the Louvre. Although the venue changed, the name Salon stayed. A jury limited the number of paintings which could be shown. In 1863 complaints about the artists rejected by the jury led to alternative exhibitions, including the Salon des Artistes Indépendants.

ACKNOWLEDGEMENTS

We would like to thank: Graham Rich, Tracey Pennington, and Peter Done for their assistance.

First published in Great Britain by *ticktock* Media Ltd., The Old Sawmill, 103 Goods Station Road, Tunbridge Wells, Kent, TN1 2DP

A CIP catalogue record for this book is available from the British Library.

ISBN 978 1 84898 043 3

Printed in China.

9 8 7 6 5 4 3 2 1

Acknowledgements: Picture Credits t=top, b=bottom, c=centre, l=left, r=right, OFC=outside front cover, IFC=inside front cover, IBC=inside back cover, OBC=outside back cover.

Art Institute of Chicago. Photo © AKG London; 10tr, 28/29cb. Christie's Images; 29br. Christie's Images/Bridgeman Art Library, London; 7tr. Courtauld Gallery, London/Bridgeman Art Library, London; 8/9t, 14tl & 24bl. David Sellman; 10/11. Fine Art Photographic Library, London; 18bl, 19tr. Groninger Museum, Groningen. Photo © AKG London; 5cr. © The Guardian (The British Library); 30/31cb. Hahnloser Collection, Bern. Photo © AKG London; IFC/1 & 16/17ct. Mary Evans Picture Library; 2tl, 2br, 3t, 3br, 28l. Metropolitan Museum of Art, New York/ Bridgeman Art Library, London; 10cr. Musee d'Orsay, Paris. Photo © AKG London/Erich Lessing; OBC & 23b, 16cl, 27br. Musee Rodin, Paris. Photo © AKG London/Erich Lessing; 8c. Musee Toulouse-Lautrec, Albi. Photo © AKG London/Erich Lessing; 6bl. Museum Folkwang, Essen. Photo © AKG London/Erich Lessing; 18cr. Museum of Modern Art, New York. Photo © AKG London; 25t. National Gallery, London/Index/Bridgeman Art Library, London; 31. National Gallery, London. Photo © AKG London/Erich Lessing; OFCl & 22bl. Photo © AKG London; 4/5cb, 15tr. Photo © Christie's/AKG London; 9cl. Private Collection/Bridgeman Art Library, London; 26tl. Private Collection, New York/Bridgeman Art Library, London; 7br. Pushkin Museum, Moscow/Bridgeman Art Library, London; 29tr. Pushkin Museum, Moscow. Photo © AKG London; 26cr. Rijksmuseum Kroeller-Mueller, Otterlo. Photo © AKG London; 11cl. Rijksmuseum Kroeller-Mueller, Otterlo. Photo © AKG London/Erich Lessing; 17br, 26tr. Rijksmuseum Vincent van Gogh, Amsterdam. Photo © AKG London; 5tl, 9cb, 30tl. Science Museum/Science & Society Picture Library; 3c. © Tate Gallery, London; 6/7cb, 12/13b, 30c. Tate Gallery, London. Photo © AKG London/Erich Lessing; 6/7ct. Van Gogh Museum (Vincent van Gogh Foundation), Amsterdam 4bl, 13tl, 13cl, 14/15bc, 15br, 18/19cb, 21t. Vincent van Gogh, Dutch, 853-1890, Self-Portrait, oil on artist's board mounted on cradled panel, 1886/87, 41 x 32.5cm, Joseph Winterbotham Collection, 1954.326, photograph © 1996, The Art Institute of Chicago. All Rights Reserved; OFCr & 11br.

Every effort has been made to trace the copyright holders and we apologise in advance for any unintentional omissions. We would be pleased to insert the appropriate acknowledgement in any subsequent edition of this publication.